Bless the Lord

1. Badgers and Hedgehogs
(*Benedicite* No. 4.)

ANDREW CARTER

O ye bad - gers and squir - rels and hedge - hogs, bless the Lord,

O ye bad - gers and squir - rels and fer - rets ___ and fox - es and hedge - hogs,

hedge - hogs, bless the Lord,

O ye

wea - sels and wart - hogs and wal - la - bies and wom - bats,

chip - munks and chuck - a - wal - las and kook - a - bur - ras and ca - ter - pil - lars and

bull - frogs and bad - gers and hedge - hogs, bless the Lord,

1 O ye pa - ra - keets and pe - li - cans and por - cu - pines and

2 O ye wea - sles and wart - hogs and wal - la - bies and

3 O ye dro - me - da - ries and ye dra - gon - flies and did - dy lit - le dad - dy -

10

2. Butterflies and Moths

(Benedicite No. 7.)

All you but-ter-flies, but-ter-flies — and moths,

all you flut-ter-ing and flit-ter-ing and fly-ing

creatures, come magnify, magnify the Lord.

All you butterflies, butterflies and moths,

all you hovering and quivering and wondrous

creatures, come magnify, magnify the Lord.

Dra-gon-flies — tremb-ling in the breeze,

la-dy-birds — ling-'ring on a flow'r, come mag-ni-fy, mag-ni-fy — the

Lord, come mag-ni-fy, mag-ni-fy — the Lord.

Kit-ti-wakes — call-ing on the cliffs,

3. Grannies and Grandads
(*Benedicite* No. 10.)

O let the earth bless the Lord

(Benedicite No. 11.)

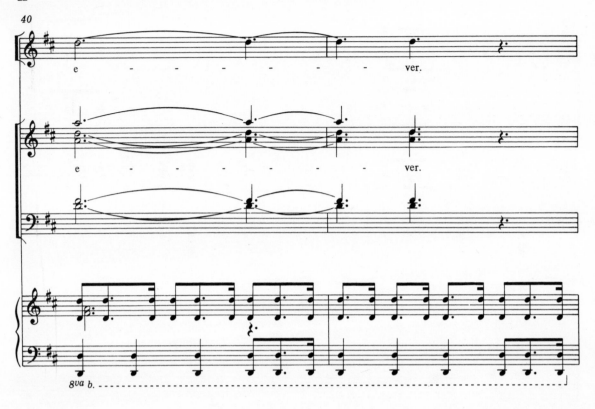

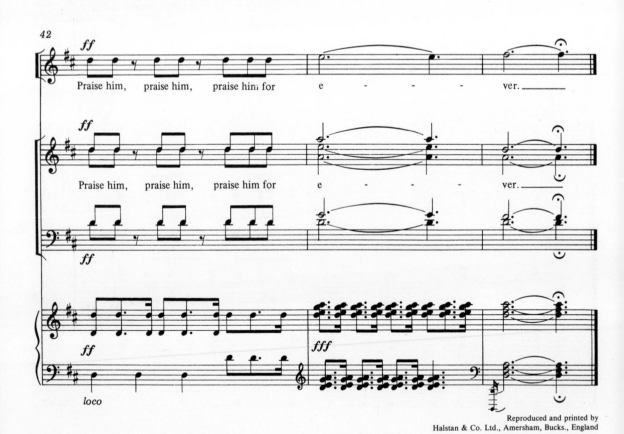

Reproduced and printed by
Halstan & Co. Ltd., Amersham, Bucks., England